D0125084

BELIEVING IN OURSELVES

The Wisdom of Women

BELIEVING IN OURSELVES

The Wisdom of Women

Ariel Books

Andrews and McMeel

Kansas City

Believing in Ourselves
The Wisdom of Women

10

ISBN: 0-8362-3015-9

Library of Congress Catalog Card Number: 91-77094

Design: Michael Hortens

BELIEVING IN
OURSELVES

The Wisdom of Women

Over the last century women have transformed their role in society tremendously. Never strangers to achievement, women are now in the corporate boardrooms and in the forefront of our politics. They are even on the frontlines of our wars. And always, regardless of the way in which they choose to contribute, women have shown a particular genius for expressing themselves.

Gathered here are thoughts and observations from some of history's most accomplished and outspoken women. Some are serious, some witty and acerbic. Each says a great deal about the remarkable character of women.

The more independent you want to be,
the more generous you must be with
yourself as a woman.

—DIANE VON FURSTENBERG

We are so vain that we even care for the
opinion of those we don't care for.

—MARIA VON EBNER-ESCHENBACH

Can you imagine a world without men?
No crime and lots of happy fat women.

—"SYLVIA" (NICOLE HOLLANDER)

Vanity is like some men, who are very
useful if they are kept under, and else
not to be endured.

—MARQUESS OF HALIFAX

The thing that makes you exceptional, if you are at all, is inevitably that which must also make you lonely.

—LORRAINE HANSBERRY

Women have served all these centuries as looking-glasses possessing the magic and delicious power of reflecting the figure of man at twice its natural size.

—VIRGINIA WOOLF

No one can make you feel inferior
without your consent.

—ELEANOR ROOSEVELT

Always be smarter than the people who
hire you.

—LENA HORNE

And what would happen to my illusion
that I am a force for order in the home if
I wasn't married to the only man north of
the Tiber who is even untidier than I am?

—KATHERINE WHITEHORN

Please know that I am aware of the hazards. I want to do it because I want to do it. Women must try to do things as men have tried. When they fail, their failure must be but a challenge to others.

—AMELIA EARHART,
IN HER LAST LETTER TO HER HUSBAND

A woman, especially if she has the misfortune of knowing anything, should conceal it as well as she can.

—JANE AUSTEN

The trouble with the rat race is that even if you win, you're still a rat.

—LILY TOMLIN

I fear nothing so much as a man who is witty all day long.

—MARQUISE DE SÉVIGNÉ

The penalty of success is to be bored by the people who used to snub you.

—LADY ASTOR

The worst part of success is to try finding someone who is happy for you.

—BETTE MIDLER

What a wonderful life I've had! I only wish I'd realized it sooner.

—COLETTE

Success is often achieved by those who don't know that failure is inevitable.

—COCO CHANEL

I blame Rousseau, myself. Man is not born free, he is born attached to his mother by a cord and is not capable of looking after himself for at least seven years (seventy in some cases).

—KATHERINE WHITEHORN

I see no reason to keep silent about my enjoyment of the sound of my own voice as I work.

—MURIEL SPARK

Think wrongly, if you please, but in all cases think for yourself.

—DORIS LESSING

I learned courage from Buddha, Jesus,
Lincoln, Einstein, and Cary Grant.

—PEGGY LEE

Don't compromise yourself. You are all
you've got.

—JANIS JOPLIN

I'll not listen to reason. . . . Reason
always means what someone else has
to say.

—ELIZABETH GASKELL

I do not know anyone who has got to
the top without hard work. That is the
recipe. It will not always get you to the
top, but should get you pretty near.

—MARGARET THATCHER

Every nation is convinced that she is dedicated to peace, but that the actions of other nations are open to suspicion. Every system of goverment is warranted by its upholders to insure harmonious relations, while every other system must lead inevitably to war.

—AGNES REPPLIER

To be successful, the first thing to do is fall in love with your work.

—SISTER MARY LAURETTA

You may be disappointed if you fail, but you are doomed if you don't try.

—BEVERLY SILLS

I do want to get rich but I never want to
do what there is to do to get rich.

—GERTRUDE STEIN

If you think you can, you can. And if
you think you can't, you're right.

—MARY KAY ASH

I invented my life by taking for granted
that everything I did not like would have
an opposite, which I would like.

—COCO CHANEL

No matter what happens, keep on
beginning and failing. Each time you fail,
start all over again, and you will grow
stronger until you find that you have
accomplished a purpose—not the one
you began with perhaps, but one you
will be glad to remember.

—ANNE SULLIVAN

One can never be too thin or too rich.

—DUCHESS OF WINDSOR
(WALLIS SIMPSON)

The idea of strictly minding our own
business is moldy rubbish. Who could be
so selfish?

—MYRTIE BARKER

Elegance is refusal.

—COCO CHANEL

When one does not know how to convince, one oppresses; in all power relations among governors and governed, as ability declines, usurpation increases.

—MADAME DE STAEL

The more I traveled the more I realized that fear makes strangers of people who should be friends.

—SHIRLEY MACLAINE

Why should we all dress after the
same fashion? The frost never paints
my windows twice alike.

—LYDIA MARIA CHILD

Because of their agelong training in
human relations—for that is what
feminine intuition really is—women have
a special contribution to make to any
group enterprise.

—MARGARET MEAD

Cruelty is a mystery,
and the waste of pain.

—ANNIE DILLARD

I keep my ideals, because in spite of
everything I still believe that people are
really good at heart.

—ANNE FRANK

I wish people wouldn't say,
"Excuse me," when I want them
to step on my feet.

—KAREN GORDON

The only thing I regret about my past
life is the length of it. If I had my
past life to do over again, I'd make all
the same mistakes—only sooner.

—TALLULAH BANKHEAD

A man in the house is worth
two in the street.

—MAE WEST

In the face of an obstacle which is
impossible to overcome, stubbornness is
stupid.

—SIMONE DE BEAUVOIR

It is not easy to find happiness in ourselves, and it is not possible to find it elsewhere.

—AGNES REPPLIER

Whatever women do they must do twice as well as men to be thought half as good. Luckily, this is not difficult.

—CHARLOTTE WHITTON

If survival depended solely on the triumph of the strong then the species would perish. So the real reason for survival, the principle factor in the "struggle of existence," is the love of adult for their young.

—MARIA MONTESSORI

. . . there are two ways to meet life; you may refuse to care until indifference becomes a habit, a defensive armor, and you are safe—but bored. Or you can care greatly, and live greatly—till life breaks you on its wheel.

—DOROTHY CANFIELD FISHER

For years I have endeavored to calm an impetuous tide—laboring to make my feelings take an orderly course—it was striving against the stream.

—MARY WOLLSTONECRAFT

I've been called many things, but never an intellectual.

—TALLULAH BANKHEAD

Remember, Ginger Rogers did everything
Fred Astaire did, but she did it
backwards and in high heels.

—FAITH WHITTLESEY

Advice is what we ask for when we
already know the answer but wish we
didn't.

—ERICA JONG

The passion for setting people right is in itself an afflictive disease.

—MARIANNE MOORE

Life's under no obligation to give us what we expect.

—MARGARET MITCHELL

If you want a thing done well, get a couple of old broads to do it.

—BETTE DAVIS

People call me a feminist whenever I express sentiments that differentiate me from a doormat or a prostitute.

—REBECCA WEST

My favorite thing is to go where I've never been.

—DIANE ARBUS

In search of my mother's garden I found my own.

—ALICE WALKER

I'm not going to limit myself just because people won't accept the fact that I can do something else.

—DOLLY PARTON

Creative minds have always been known to survive any kind of bad training.

—ANNA FREUD

I think these difficult times have helped
me to understand better than before how
infinitely rich and beautiful life is in
every way and that so many things that
one goes around worrying about are of
no importance whatsoever.

—ISAK DINESEN

I feel like I'm fighting a battle when I didn't start a war.

—DOLLY PARTON

One is not born a woman, one becomes one.

—SIMONE DE BEAUVOIR

It is not true that life is one damn thing
after another . . . it's the same damn
thing over and over again.

—EDNA ST. VINCENT MILLAY

The most courageous act is still to think
for yourself. Aloud.

—COCO CHANEL

The main dangers in this life are the
people who want to change everything
. . . or nothing.

—LADY ASTOR

Fate keeps happening.

—ANITA LOOS

Nobody has ever measured, even poets,
how much the heart can hold.

—ZELDA FITZGERALD

It is a general mistake to think the men we like are good for everything, and those we do not, good for nothing.

—MARQUESS OF HALIFAX

I don't know why women want any of the things that men have when one of the things that women have is men.

—COCO CHANEL

Oh, seek, my love, your newer way; I'll
not be left in sorrow. So long as I have
yesterday, go take your damned
tomorrow!

—DOROTHY PARKER

There is a time for work. And a time for
love. That leaves no other time.

—COCO CHANEL

Trust your husband, adore your husband, and get as much as you can in your own name.

—JOAN RIVERS

The way I see it, if you want the rainbow, you gotta put up with the rain.

—DOLLY PARTON

Ultimately, love is self-approval.

—SONDRA RAY

If the world were a logical place, men would ride side-saddle.

—RITA MAE BROWN

It is flattering some men to endure them.

—MARQUESS OF HALIFAX

Love and a cough
cannot be concealed.
Even a small cough
Even a small love.

—ANNE SEXTON

Men do not think of sons and daughters,
when they fall in love.

—ELIZABETH BARRETT BROWNING

No artist is ahead of his time. He is the time. It is just that others are behind the time.

—MARTHA GRAHAM

I wrote the story myself. It's all about a girl who lost her reputation but never missed it.

—MAE WEST

If pregnancy were a book they would
cut out the last two chapters.

—NORA EPHRON

Culture is an instrument wielded by
professors to manufacture professors,
who when their turn comes, will
manufacture professors.

—SIMONE WEIL

One old lady who wants her head lifted wouldn't be so bad, but you multiply her two hundred and fifty thousand times and what you get is a book club.

—FLANNERY O'CONNOR

In heaven they will bore you, in hell you will bore them.

—KATHERINE WHITEHORN

The tombstone is about the only thing that can stand upright and lie on its face at the same time.

—MARY WILSON LITTLE

No one can build his (sic) security upon the nobleness of another person.

—WILLA CATHER

If I lead another life in any of the
planets, I shall take precious good care
not to hang myself around any man's
neck either as a locket or a millstone.

—JANE CARLYLE

She always believed in the old adage—
leave them while you're
looking good.

—ANITA LOOS

Prejudices, it is well known, are most difficult to eradicate from the heart whose soil has never been loosened or fertilized by education; they grow firm there, firm as weeds among stones.

—CHARLOTTE BRONTË

Whenever I'm caught between two evils, I take the one I haven't tried yet.

—MAE WEST

51

Lack of education is an extraordinary handicap when one is being offensive.

—JOSEPHINE TEY

To suffer is to be alone; to watch another suffer is to know the barrier that shuts each of us away. Only individuals can suffer.

—EDITH HAMILTON

I don't have a warm personal enemy left.
They've all died off. I miss them terribly
because they helped define me.

—CLARE BOOTHE LUCE

Parenthood: that state of being better
chaperoned than you were before
marriage.

—MADELINE COX

Too often, I think, children are required to write before they have anything to say. Teach them to think and read and talk without self-repression, and they will write because they cannot help it.

—ANNE SULLIVAN

If it were natural for fathers to care for their sons, they would not need so many laws commanding them to do so.

—PHYLLIS CHESLER

How sad that man would base an entire civilization on the principle of paternity, upon legal ownership and presumed responsibility for children, and then never really get to know their sons and daughters very well.

—PHYLLIS CHESLER

Egotism—usually a case of mistaken nonentity.

—BARBARA STANWYCK

A man finds out what is meant
by a spitting image when he tries to feed
cereal to his infant.

—IMOGENE FEY

Sometimes when I look at
my children I say to myself, "Lillian,
you should have stayed a virgin."

—LILLIAN CARTER

There is glory in a great mistake.

—NATHALIA CRANE

Father's birthday. He would have been
96 years old today; and could have
been 96, like other people one has
known; mercifully was not. His life
would have utterly ended mine.

—VIRGINIA WOOLF

Fortune does not change men,
it unmasks them.

—SUZANNE NECKER

Grief is so selfish.

—MARY ELIZABETH BRADDON

If we'd only stop trying to be happy
we'd have a pretty good time.

—EDITH WHARTON

Happiness is good health and
a bad memory.

—INGRID BERGMAN

Real solemn history, I cannot be interested in. The quarrels of popes and kings, with wars and pestilences in every page; the men so good for nothing, and hardly any women at all.

—JANE AUSTEN

Opportunities are usually disguised as hard work, so most people don't recognize them.

—ANN LANDERS

Every major horror of history was
committed in the name of an altruistic
motive. Has any act of selfishness ever
equalled the carnage perpetuated by
disciples of altruism?

—AYN RAND

When the freedom they wished for most
was freedom from responsibility, then
Athens ceased to be free and was never
free again.

—EDITH HAMILTON

I prefer the word "homemaker" because "housewife" always implies that there may be a wife someplace else.

—BELLA ABZUG

Only the untalented can afford to be humble.

—SYLVIA MILES

I have yet to hear a man ask for
advice on how to combine marriage
and a career.

— GLORIA STEINEM

A man's home may seem to be his castle
on the outside; inside, it is more often
his nursery.

— CLARE BOOTHE LUCE

62

Before you can drive a car you need a state-approved course of instruction, but driving a car is nothing, nothing, compared to living day in and day out with a husband and raising up a new human being.

—ANNE TYLER

A hurtful act is the transference to others of the degradation which we bear on ourselves.

—SIMONE WEIL

Jealousy is no more than feeling alone
against smiling enemies.

—ELIZABETH BOWEN

I find the public passion for justice
quite boring and artificial, for neither
life nor nature cares if justice is ever
done or not.

—PATRICIA HIGHSMITH

I have bursts of being a lady,
but it doesn't last long.

—SHELLEY WINTERS

He who laughs, lasts.

—MARY PETTIBONE POOLE

Good women are no fun. The only good
woman I can recall in history is Betsy
Ross. And all she ever made was a flag.

—MAE WEST

Nothing is so good as it seems
to be beforehand.

—GEORGE ELIOT

There are only two or three human
stories, and they go on repeating
themselves as fiercely as if they had
never happened before.

—WILLA CATHER

Nothing seems so tragic to one
who is old as the death of one who
is young, and this alone proves
that life is a good thing.

—ZOE ATKINS

The one thing I regret is that
I will never have time to read all the
books I want to read.

—FRANÇOISE SAGAN

Don't threaten me with love, baby.
Let's just go walking in the rain.

—BILLIE HOLIDAY

Love is the extremely difficult
realization that something other than
oneself is real.

—IRIS MURDOCH

People talk about love as though it were something you could give, like an armful of flowers.

—ANNE MORROW LINDBERGH

To love without criticism is to be betrayed.

—DJUNA BARNES

In the arithmetic of love, one plus one equals everything, and two minus one equals nothing.

—MIGNON MCLAUGHLIN

Millions long for immortality who do not
know what to do with themselves on a
rainy Sunday afternoon.

—SUSAN ERTZ

Never marry a man who
hates his mother because he'll end up
hating you.

—JILL BENNETT

Marrying a man is like buying something you've been admiring for a long time in a shop window. You may love it when you get it home, but it doesn't always go with everything else in the house.

—JEAN KERR

Everybody gets so much information all day long that they lose their common sense.

—GERTRUDE STEIN

I have always felt that a woman has the right to treat the subject of her age with ambiguity until, perhaps, she passes into the realm of over ninety. Then it is better she be candid with herself and with the world.

—HELENA RUBINSTEIN

But old women are different from everybody else; they say what they think.

—URSULA LE GUIN

Intimacies between women
often go backwards, beginning in
revelations and ending in small
talk without loss of esteem.

—ELIZABETH BOWEN

Sometimes I think if there was a third sex
men wouldn't get so much as a glance
from me.

—AMANDA VAIL

All the men on my staff can type.

—BELLA ABZUG

The male is a domestic animal
which, if treated with firmness and
kindness, can be trained to do
most things.

— MILLY COOPER

Beware of men who cry.
It's true that men who cry are sensitive to
and in touch with feelings, but the only
feelings they tend to be sensitive to and
in touch with are their own.

— NORA EPHRON

I don't mind how much my ministers
talk—as long as they do what I say.

—MARGARET THATCHER

It's a man's world,
and you men can have it.

—KATHERINE ANNE PORTER

Why are women so much more
interesting to men than men are to
women?

—VIRGINIA WOOLF

Women speak because they wish
to speak, whereas a man speaks only
when driven to speech by
something outside himself—like,
for instance, he can't find any
clean socks.

—JEAN KERR

Men are generally more law-abiding than women. Women have the feeling that since they didn't make the rules, the rules have nothing to do with them.

—DIANE JOHNSON

A phenomenon noticeable throughout history regardless of place or period is the pursuit by governments of policies contrary to their own interest.

—BARBARA TUCHMAN

Your can't shake hands with a clenched fist.

—INDIRA GANDHI

Just the knowledge that a good book is
awaiting one at the end of a long day
makes that day happier.

—KATHLEEN NORRIS

The great thing about getting older is
that you don't lose all the other ages
you've been.

—MADELINE L'ENGLE

The text of this book was set in
Garamond Book by
Trufont Typographers, Inc.
Hicksville, New York

Designed by Michael Hortens

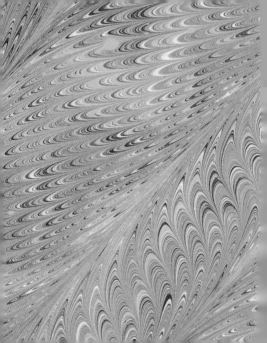